Will I Ever Be Good Enough?

Words by
Judith Conaway

Pictures by
Bruce Witty

Raintree Editions

Design/Paul Westermann

Library of Congress Number: 76-45854

2 3 4 5 6 7 8 9 0 81 80 79 78

Printed in the United States of America.

Published by

Raintree Editions
A Division of Raintree Publishers Limited
Milwaukee, Wisconsin 53203

Distributed by

Childrens Press
1224 West Van Buren Street
Chicago, Illinois 60607

Library of Congress Cataloging in Publication Data

Conaway, Judith.
Will I ever be good enough?

SUMMARY: A young girl develops self-confidence in her own abilities and overcomes the envy she feels toward her friend.
1. Competition (Psychology) — Juvenile literature. 2. Self-acceptance — Juvenile literature. [1. Self-acceptance] I. Witty, Bruce. II. Title.
BF683.C655 158'.1 76-45854
ISBN 0-8172-0059-2

15
The Golden Treasury of
KNOWLEDGE
FLOWERS

My teacher says that if you want to know a lot, you have to read books. I want to know about everything in the whole world. So I'm going to read every single one of these books. After I've read them, I will read all the other books in the library. Then I will be very smart.

Maybe I will get to be smart enough to be an important scientist. When I am a scientist, I will walk around writing things down in a great big notebook. Scientists are always doing that.

Maybe I will find a new kind of plant. I will study the plant for years and years. I will make lots of notes. Then I will make a great discovery. I will find a new way to make medicine from the plant. Hospitals all over the world will use my medicine. I will be famous.

Oh, dear. The words in this book are hard. I can't read them too well. What will I do? A scientist has to know how to read millions of words. How will I ever be good enough to be a scientist?

omatic mints are also
Horsemint. They vary
vender. The brilliant
moist places, but the
nd fencerows. Some
ers, brought from
e wild. Indians and
wed medicinal tea
-Summer and early
TRILLIUMS Trilliums are handsome spring plants of moist eastern woodlands and western mountains. As their name implies, they are constructed on a threefold plan: 3 leaflets, 3 green sepals, and 3 petals which vary in color from the deep, purple-red of the common Wake-robin through pink to pure white. There are about 15 species—most grow a foot or so high, usually in rich soil. The flowers ripen into reddish or purple berries.—Spring. Lily Family.
15 species

Maybe I should be an explorer instead. I will find places where no one has ever been before. I will go deep into the jungle. The jungle will be full of strange noises. Wild animals will be hiding behind the bushes. But I won't be afraid. I will keep on going. I will find secret cities and lost kingdoms. Then my name will be in the newspapers. People will ask me to be on television.

Or maybe I will be a model. I will wear a long black dress. I will be very beautiful. My picture will be on all the magazine covers.

Why don't I just give up? Look at this face. Of course, it might get better when I'm older. But will I ever be pretty enough to be a model?

Now, Meg could be a model. She's so pretty. Everyone says so.

Maybe I will be a photographer. I will travel all over the world to take pictures. Or maybe I will make movies. I wonder if I could learn to take pictures.

Meg is really lucky. She is pretty and smart. She can do almost anything. She wins all the contests at school. Everyone says that someday Meg will be in the Olympics.

I wish I were Meg. I wish I were pretty and smart. I wish I could be in the Olympics.

I would leap high into the air. I would make a perfect landing. I would flip over and over. I would move very fast. I would never make any mistakes.

People would say, “How does she do it? Isn’t she wonderful?”

I would win all the gold medals at the Olympics. The people would clap and cheer for me. The reporters would come up and ask me questions.

But what's the use? I'll never be good enough for the Olympics. It's too hard. Sometimes it seems as if everything is too hard. There are so many things I can't do. Will I ever be good enough to be a scientist or an explorer or a photographer? Will I ever be good enough to be anything at all?

Guess what? Meg is helping me with my gymnastics. We started today. The first thing we did was somersaults. They were really easy. I did one on the first try. But then we had to keep doing somersaults over and over. We must have done somersaults for a whole hour. Meg says that's the way to learn. You have to practice the simple tricks until you are really good.

Then you can go on to the harder tricks. Every day you practice a little bit more. It gets easier all the time. That's because your body is getting used to the extra work.

Meg and I practice together every day now. We're both getting to be pretty good. We help each other. Sometimes, when we practice, we pretend we are in the Olympics. Thousands of people are watching us. Everyone is cheering and yelling. We are the stars.

Will we ever be good enough to be in the Olympics? I don't know. But I know we're going to try hard.

I'm so glad I have Meg for a friend. We do lots of things together. Right now I'm showing Meg how to crochet. My mom taught me when I was little, but Meg never learned. Now she's getting good at it. Pretty soon she will be good enough to make a sweater.

One thing I like about Meg is that she is never afraid to try new things. The other day, Meg read a book about airplanes. Now she says that she wants to be a pilot. She says becoming a pilot will be hard work. It will take years and years.

I wonder if I could ever be good enough to fly a plane? You know, if I really wanted to, I think I could.